SHAKESPEARE FOR EVERYONE

THE TEMPEST

By Jennifer Mulherin and Abigail Frost
Illustrations by George Thompson
CHERRYTREE BOOKS

Author's note

There is no substitute for seeing the plays of Shakespeare performed. Only then can you really understand why Shakespeare is our greatest dramatist and poet. This book simply gives you the background to the play and tells you about the story and characters. It will, I hope, encourage you to see the play.

A Cherrytree Book

Designed and produced by
A S Publishing

First published 1992
by Cherrytree Press Ltd
a subsidiary of
The Chivers Company Ltd
Windsor Bridge Road
Bath, Avon BA2 3AX

British Library Cataloguing in Publication Data

Mulherin, Jennifer
  The Tempest
  I. Title II. Series III. Frost, Abigail
  822.3'3

ISBN 0-7451-5168-X

Typesetting by Image Typographics, London
Printed in Hong Kong by Colorcraft Ltd

Contents

O brave new world!

A seventeenth-century map of Virginia, showing (inset) Powhatan, the Indian chief who at first befriended John Smith.

In 1609 nine ships set sail from England to America. They were taking people and supplies (such as flour, cloth and guns) to the British colony called Virginia, on the coast of the modern state of that name. But a hurricane blew up, and

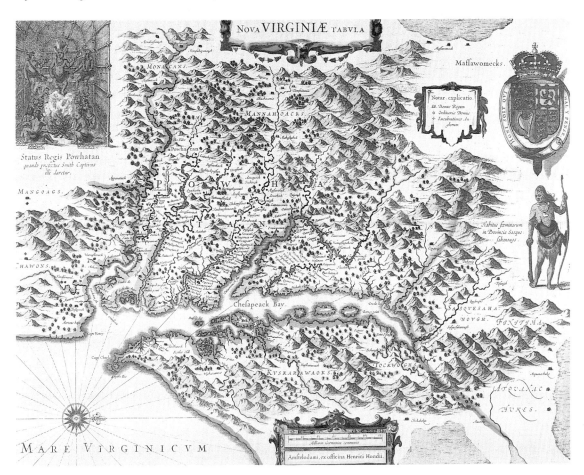

one ship, the *Sea Venture,* commanded by Sir George Somers, was wrecked on one of a group of uninhabited islands. These islands – the Bermudas – were thought to be haunted by evil spirits: Sir William Strachey, who was on the ship, wrote that they were known as 'The Devil's Islands', and 'feared and avoided of all sea travellers alive, above any other place in the world'

The castaways soon found, however, that the island was 'abundantly fruitful', though it had no fresh water except for rain. (They probably had their own water in barrels on the ship, which was wedged between two rocks.) To eat they found wild pigs, turtles ('such a kind of meat, as a man can neither absolutely call Fish nor Flesh'), the local sea-birds ('a good and well relished Fowl, full and fat as a Partridge') and cedarberries and other fruits. The voyagers stayed for nine months, while they built boats to take them and their remaining supplies on to Virginia. Two children had been born on the island, and christened Bermuda and Bermudas.

Hard times in Virginia

The colonists on the other ships had, meanwhile, arrived safely in Virginia. But they had not fared as well as Somers's party. After a terrible winter they had only four days' supply of food left when the boats arrived from the Bermudas in May 1610. They had survived only because of their determined leader, Captain John Smith, and the help of local Indians with whom he made friends and traded goods. But Smith had left the colony and headed north (to the lands that he named New England) after quarrels with less-disciplined colleagues.

This fanciful German engraving shows Amerigo Vespucci encountering the weird and wonderful inhabitants of the continent that was to be named after him.

The Indians had shown the colonists how to cultivate local plants (such as 'Indian corn', or sweetcorn), and how to trap fish in the fast-flowing rivers by 'damming' them with sticks – but the colonists (many of whom had hoped to find a 'land of gold' rather than a hard farming life) never became as skilled as their teachers. And some of the Indians had become hostile. Things were so bad that Somers and his shipmates had almost decided to return to England when another ship arrived, with enough supplies to save the colonists from starvation.

Shakespeare's America

Shakespeare knew some of the people who paid for the voyages to Virginia, and may even have known Sir William Strachey. Many details in *The Tempest* are based on Strachey's account of the wreck. Ariel's fiery dance in the ship's rigging (see page 13) is St Elmo's Fire, a type of lightning that Strachey saw on the *Sea Venture:* 'A little round light, like a faint Star, trembling, and streaming along with a sparkling blaze … and shooting sometimes from Shroud to Shroud … running sometimes along the Main-yard to the very end, and then returning.' The idea of an island inhabited by spirits, and 'full of noises', as Caliban says, comes from the sailors' superstitions about Bermuda, though Strachey pours cold water on them.

Indian ways

Other details, especially those about Caliban, come from life in colonial Virginia. Like the Indians, Caliban taught Prospero to survive in his new home, showing him which plants were good to eat and damming rivers to catch fish; and like them, he soon regretted handing over his land to a stranger. He was angry at being exploited by a person who was unwilling to do the hard work for himself.

American Indians trapping and spearing fish in Virginia. Without their help, the early colonists would not have survived.

Shakespeare's magic

When Shakespeare's audience first met Prospero and his mysterious 'Art', they would have thought of Dr John Dee, a scientist, astrologer and magician who had died two years before.

In Shakespeare's day, all but a few sceptics believed in magic, in horoscopes or simply in 'luck'. Country girls would cast spells to find out their future husbands' names. Builders would kill a cat or chicken and bury it in the foundations of a new house to ward off evil spirits. Even Queen Elizabeth I had believed in horoscopes, and John Dee was her personal astrologer.

Dee did much more than cast the royal horoscope. He was an alchemist, obsessed with finding the 'philosopher's stone', a mysterious substance that would, people believed, turn lead into gold. Like Prospero, he conjured up spirits (or thought he did). He believed his secret knowledge, learned from magic books and conversations with spirits, would eventually give him power over the whole world – including the spirit world.

The magician deceived
Luckily, perhaps, Dee did not succeed. In fact, most of his 'successful' experiments were faked (without his knowledge) by his assistant, Edward Kelly. Kelly lived very well at the expense of Dee and various European princes who employed them, so it paid him to go on fooling Dee by speaking in 'spirit voices' or slipping pieces of gold into his chemical apparatus. Eventually the two quarrelled, and Dee left Kelly in Bohemia (now Czechoslovakia) and returned to England, where the queen herself welcomed him.

Magic mathematics

Dee had many methods of contacting spirits. He used a 'magic mirror', which was actually an Aztec object, brought from Mexico by Spanish conquistadors (conquerors), and a 'magic stone' (or crystal ball), both of which still exist. He also believed that numbers had magical power, and that spirits could be raised by certain mathematical calculations. His interest in mathematics had more practical uses than his magic: he wrote about geometry and helped map-makers, navigators, architects and gunsmiths, among others, with his expertise.

John Dee, like most alchemists and magicians, was also a serious scholar. He had the finest library in England, with over 4000 books.

Stage magic

Dee even used his talents on stage. As a young man, he designed a 'flying machine' for a Greek play put on at Trinity College, Cambridge; it carried a man up to the roof. It was purely mechanical, but it caused many people to suspect Dee of 'black arts' for the first time.

By the time *The Tempest* was performed, nearly 50 years later, people were used to spectacular stage effects. Even on open stages with no electric light or amplified sound, an enormous range of illusions was possible, using machines, sound-effects, trap-doors and gunpowder. *The Tempest* offers many opportunities.

Thunder for the storm could be created by rolling a bullet over a metal sheet in the 'heavens' (a room in the roof over the stage). For lightning, Shakespeare's company probably used fireworks: they were certainly used in his friend Christopher Marlowe's *Dr Faustus*, where, it was said, 'a man might behold shag-haired devils run roaring over the Stage with Squibs in their mouths ... and the twelve-penny Hirelings make artificial lightning in their Heavens'. Gunpowder was also used (not in *The Tempest*) to fire real cannon in battle or ceremonial scenes: in 1613 the Globe

Edward Kelly summons up the spirit of a newly-dead man to ask him about some hidden money. Kelly was so skilled a hoaxer that his clients paid him handsomely.

Theatre caught fire when cannons were fired in Shakespeare's *Henry VIII*.

Some scenes required more complex preparations. How was the banquet in Act III Scene iii made to disappear? There is no record, but scholars have made suggestions based on known facts about Shakespeare's stage. The table (with the food on it) might have risen from a trap-door, with a stage-hand hiding under the table-cloth. When Ariel raised his wings (and hid the table from sight), the stage-hand could pull the cloth and food down through a secret panel in the table-top, and leave by the trap-door. Another suggestion is that the table-top might be reversible, with the banquet dishes nailed to one side and the other showing a bare cloth. Again, the transformation would take place when Ariel's wings made a screen. A hanging cloth could cover the dishes underneath.

Masques

The taste for spectacle had grown with the court fashion for masques. These were entertainments based on music and dancing, performed by the king or queen and courtiers themselves, to mark special occasions, such as weddings. They often had elaborate scenery and costumes designed by the architect Inigo Jones. Special effects, such as live gods and goddesses appearing out of painted clouds, were a feature of Jones's masque designs.

Shakespeare's company could not afford anything so complicated. Masque settings took several days to build, during which the performing area could not be used for anything else. Professional actors had to perform every day, because they lived on the takings. But the company obviously learned a lot from the court designers and carpenters, and sometimes (as in *The Tempest*) introduced miniature masques into their own plays.

Prospero's Books – *a modern film version of* The Tempest – *employed spectacular effects to create Prospero's magic.*

The story of The Tempest

Far out on a stormy sea, a ship is in grave danger. The master and boatswain shout across the deck as the crew haul down the sails. Then some great lords – the ship's passengers – come on deck, and soon start to interfere. The short-tempered boatswain tells them to go below and say their prayers. As the crew try to save the ship the haughty lords go back to their king's quarters.

Fear
Now would I give a thousand furlongs of sea for an acre of barren ground; long heath, brown furze, any thing. The wills above be done! but I would fain die a dry death.
Act I Sc i

Prospero's tale

They are watched, unknown to them, by the people of a nearby island. The beautiful Miranda begs her father, the magician Prospero, to calm the storm – which he has raised – to save the ship and the people aboard. Her father says there is nothing to worry about – he has magically brought the ship safe to land. Now he asks what she can remember of her past, and tells her the story of how they both came to be living on the island.

Twelve years before, when Miranda was a small child, Prospero was Duke of Milan, a rich Italian city. But Prospero spent his time studying magic and left the government of the city to his brother Antonio. Antonio cheated him and at last, helped by Alonso, King of Naples, had his brother banished. Prospero and his tiny daughter were set adrift in a leaky boat.

Exile

In few, they hurried us aboard a bark,
Bore us some leagues to sea; where they prepar'd
A rotten carcass of a boat, not rigg'd,
Nor tackle, sail, nor mast; the very rats
Instinctively have quit it: there they hoist us,
To cry to the sea that roar'd to us; to sigh
To the winds whose pity, sighing back again,
Did us but loving wrong.

Act I Sc ii

But Gonzalo, a lord of Naples, made sure they had food, clothes and Prospero's magic books which helped them survive until they landed on this island.

A single chance

Now, Prospero tells Miranda, his life is about to take a turn. According to the stars, he must grasp his chance of luck or, for ever after, things will go badly. Miranda falls asleep before he can tell her what this chance is.

Prospero calls his spirit-servant, Ariel, to tell him about the storm. Ariel has enjoyed frightening the lords and sailors with his tricks, turning himself into flames and thunder-

St Elmo's fire

I boarded the king's ship; now on the beak,
Now in the waist, the deck, in every cabin,
I flam'd amazement: sometime I'd divide
And burn in many places; on the topmast,
The yards, and boresprit, would I flame distinctly,
Then meet, and join: Jove's lightnings, the precursors
O' the dreadful thunder-claps, more momentary
And sight-outrunning were not: the fire and cracks
Of sulphurous roaring the most mighty Neptune
Seem to besiege and make his bold waves tremble,
Yea, his dread trident shake.

Act I Sc ii

bolts in the rigging. But he finally brought the ship safely to harbour, and led the passengers ashore in groups, except for the king's son Ferdinand, whom he left alone on a bank.

Among the lords on the ship were Prospero's enemies, the King of Naples (Alonso) and Antonio. They were returning from Alonso's daughter's wedding in Tunis. With them were Gonzalo, who had helped Prospero, and the king's son Ferdinand. Prospero has halted their journey to win his dukedom back.

Ariel's duty

Prospero thanks Ariel for his good work – but there is more to be done. Ariel protests: a year ago his master had promised to set him free now. Prospero angrily reminds Ariel how he saved him: the poor spirit had been imprisoned in a tree by a witch called Sycorax, who had died and left him there, with no company but her son Caliban. If Ariel complains any more, Prospero will put him back in the tree: but if he serves willingly, he will be freed very soon. Ariel must make himself invisible, like a water-nymph, and fetch Ferdinand.

An unwilling slave

Miranda awakens and Prospero takes her to visit Caliban, now his slave. She is reluctant to go, saying she hates to see him. Caliban, when called, is bad-tempered: 'There's wood enough within!' he cries from his cave. But Prospero calls him out – he has work other than wood-gathering for the witch's son. Caliban curses Prospero, who threatens him in return. Caliban goes on complaining: 'I must eat my dinner'. He thinks he has been hard-done-by: when Prospero arrived, he was kind to Caliban, who showed him over the island. Now he is a slave. Prospero says this is his punishment for trying to rape Miranda. This is the real reason why she hates him so.

A cruel master

Cal. *You taught me language; and my profit on't*
      Is, I know how to curse: the red plague rid you,
      For learning me your language!

Pro. *Hag-seed, hence!*
      Fetch us in fuel; and be quick, thou'rt best,
      To answer other business. Shrug'st thou, malice?
      If thou neglect'st, or dost unwillingly
      What I command, I'll rack thee with old cramps,
      Fill all thy bones with aches; make thee roar,
      That beasts shall tremble at thy din.

                                  Act I Sc ii

Love at first sight

Ariel, meanwhile, has found Ferdinand, and led him with magical singing to Prospero's cell. His song reminds Ferdinand of his dead father. Prospero turns Miranda away from Caliban's cave, and asks what she thinks of the prince. 'What is't? A spirit?' she asks, overwhelmed by the sight of him – she cannot remember seeing any man but her father and the hideous Caliban. Ferdinand takes her for a goddess, but Prospero stops his compliments, and mentions the King of Naples. Ferdinand, assuming his father has drowned, says he is King of Naples now. Prospero does not reveal his own identity. He calls Ferdinand a usurper, and claims him as a slave. Ferdinand draws his sword – but Prospero's magic freezes him in mid-movement. Miranda begs her father not to hurt Ferdinand. Prospero, who realises the two have fallen in love, brushes aside her pleas.

Alonso's grief

On another part of the island, Alonso and his lords are talking about their escape from drowning. Old Gonzalo tries to comfort the king, who thinks his son is dead. Antonio and the king's cynical brother Sebastian mock the old man's pompous way of speaking. But another lord, Adrian, also tries to cheer the king, pointing out how pleasant the island seems. Antonio and Sebastian jeer – where Gonzalo points out green grass, they say the ground is 'tawny'.

Gonzalo presses on: the greatest wonder, he says, is the state of their clothes. Despite everything, they are as fresh and dry as they were when they were put on in Tunis! Antonio and Sebastian go on mocking, until the king can bear no more. His son is drowned, and his daughter now lives far away. Lord Francisco says he saw Ferdinand swimming away from the wreck. Perhaps he is alive. But Alonso will not listen.

Sea-change song

Full fathom five thy father lies;
  Of his bones are coral made:
Those are pearls that were eyes:
  Nothing of him that doth fade,
But doth suffer a sea-change
Into something rich and strange.
Sea-nymphs hourly ring his knell:
    Burden: ding-dong.
Hark! now I hear them, – ding-dong, bell.

Act I Sc ii

Miranda falls in love
What is't? a spirit?
Lord, how it looks about! Believe me, sir,
It carries a brave form:– but 'tis a spirit.

Act I Sc ii

Mockery

The air breathes upon us here most sweetly.
Seb.   *As if it had lungs, and rotten ones.*
Ant.   *Or as 'twere perfumed by a fen.*
Gon.   *Here is everything advantageous to life.*
Ant.   *True; save means to live.*
Seb.   *Of that there's none, or little.*
Gon.   *How lush and lusty the grass looks! how green!*
Ant.   *The ground indeed is tawny.*
Seb.   *With an eye of green in't.*

Act II Sc i

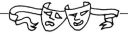

An ideal kingdom

Changing the subject, Gonzalo says what he would do if he ruled an island like this one: there would be no war, no one rich or poor, and all nature's gifts would be shared equally. While the cynical lords mock him, Ariel enters. His magic music puts them all to sleep – except for Antonio and Sebastian. As the king dozes off, these two promise to guard him.

Gonzalo's ideal world

All things in common nature should produce
Without sweat or endeavour: treason, felony,
Sword, pike, knife, gun, or need of any engine,
Would I not have; but nature should bring forth,
Of its own kind, all foison, all abundance,
To feed my innocent people.

Act II Sc i

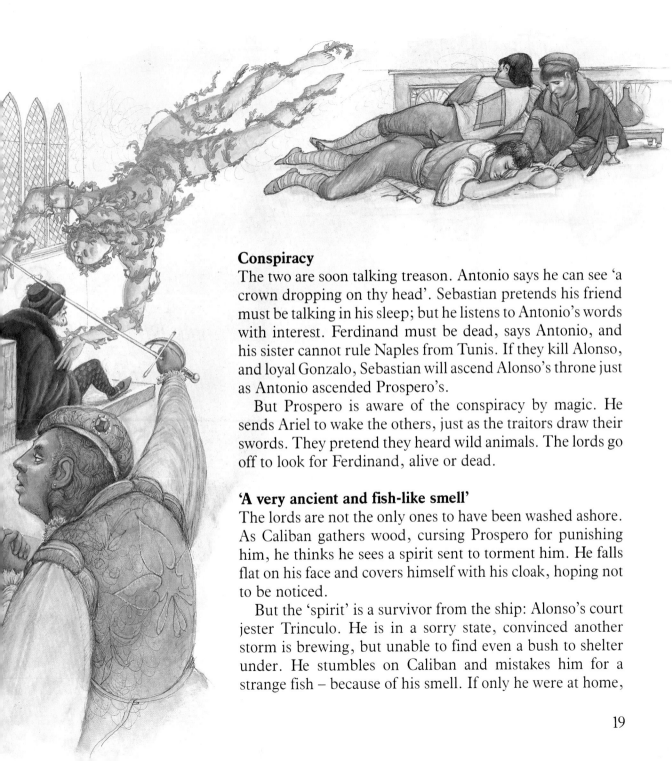

Conspiracy

The two are soon talking treason. Antonio says he can see 'a crown dropping on thy head'. Sebastian pretends his friend must be talking in his sleep; but he listens to Antonio's words with interest. Ferdinand must be dead, says Antonio, and his sister cannot rule Naples from Tunis. If they kill Alonso, and loyal Gonzalo, Sebastian will ascend Alonso's throne just as Antonio ascended Prospero's.

But Prospero is aware of the conspiracy by magic. He sends Ariel to wake the others, just as the traitors draw their swords. They pretend they heard wild animals. The lords go off to look for Ferdinand, alive or dead.

'A very ancient and fish-like smell'

The lords are not the only ones to have been washed ashore. As Caliban gathers wood, cursing Prospero for punishing him, he thinks he sees a spirit sent to torment him. He falls flat on his face and covers himself with his cloak, hoping not to be noticed.

But the 'spirit' is a survivor from the ship: Alonso's court jester Trinculo. He is in a sorry state, convinced another storm is brewing, but unable to find even a bush to shelter under. He stumbles on Caliban and mistakes him for a strange fish – because of his smell. If only he were at home,

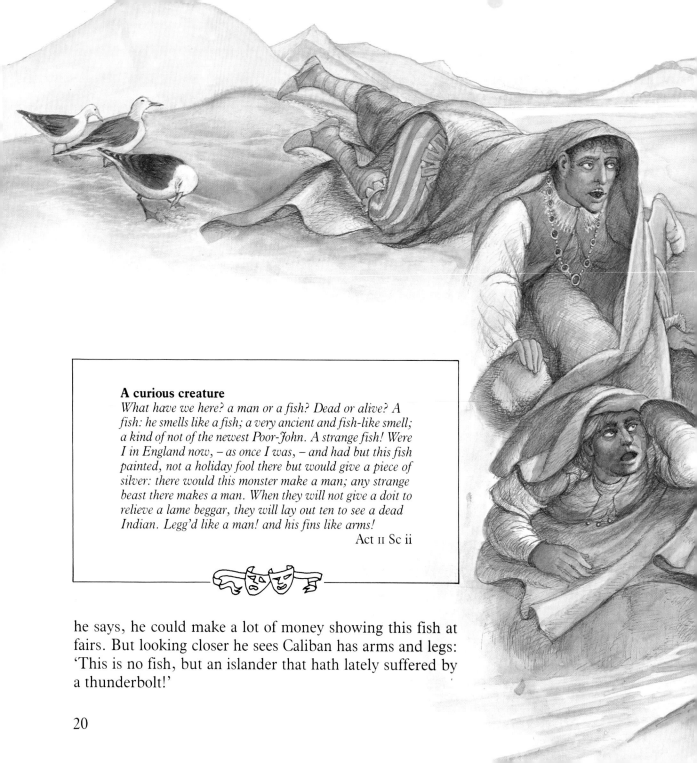

A curious creature

What have we here? a man or a fish? Dead or alive? A fish: he smells like a fish; a very ancient and fish-like smell; a kind of not of the newest Poor-John. A strange fish! Were I in England now, – as once I was, – and had but this fish painted, not a holiday fool there but would give a piece of silver: there would this monster make a man; any strange beast there makes a man. When they will not give a doit to relieve a lame beggar, they will lay out ten to see a dead Indian. Legg'd like a man! and his fins like arms!

Act II Sc ii

he says, he could make a lot of money showing this fish at fairs. But looking closer he sees Caliban has arms and legs: 'This is no fish, but an islander that hath lately suffered by a thunderbolt!'

20

Caliban's new master

A clap of thunder sends Trinculo scurrying under Caliban's cloak. Along comes Stephano, the king's butler, who has rescued the king's wine from the shipwreck. He is drunkenly singing sea-shanties. Caliban cries out, thinking Trinculo has come to hurt him, and Stephano thinks he has found a monster that he can sell to a rich lord.

Hoping to tame the beast, he gives Caliban some wine. Trinculo recognises him and calls out. For a moment, Stephano thinks the monster has 'four legs and two voices', but he soon recognises his friend. While they exchange escape-stories, Caliban – drunk for the first time in his life – staggers about. He thinks Stephano, who rescued him from the 'spirit' and gave him such a wonderful drink, is a god. He promises to serve him, and just as he did for Prospero years ago, show him the best spots on the island.

A friendly native
I prithee, let me bring thee where crabs grow;
And I with my long nails will dig thee pig-nuts;
Show thee a jay's nest and instruct thee how
To snare the nimble marmozet; I'll bring thee
To clust'ring filberts, and sometimes I'll get thee
Young scamels from the rock.

Act II Sc ii

Lovers' vows

Ferdinand has been working too, piling up heavy logs. But thoughts of Miranda make his task bearable. She comes to his side and begs him to rest, saying her father is safely away studying. She even offers to carry the wood for him, But he refuses.

Ferdinand says that though he is a prince – a king, even –

he will be a 'patient log-man' for Miranda. She asks if he loves her and when he says yes, says she will marry him – if he wants her to.

But Prospero is watching them unseen. As they confess their love for each other, he is glad; the time is nearly right for him to free Ferdinand.

Ariel stirs things up

Caliban and his drunken companions explore the island. Trinculo and Caliban soon start to quarrel. Caliban says the jester is not as good as his new master, Stephano. Stephano warns Trinculo against mutiny – the drink and Caliban's adoration are going to his head. Ariel, still invisible, enters. He decides to have some fun.

While Caliban tells Stephano about the 'tyrant' he serves, Ariel adds 'Thou liest'. Stephano tells Trinculo he will knock his teeth out if he interrupts Caliban. 'Why, I said nothing,' says the jester. As Caliban continues, Ariel breaks in again. Stephano turns on Trinculo: 'Didst thou not say he lied?'

'Thou liest,' says Ariel, and Stephano starts to beat Trinculo. But he wants to hear the rest of Caliban's story. The slave says Prospero always sleeps in the afternoon. That would be a good time to kill him, and steal his magic books. Then Stephano could rule the island and marry Miranda.

As they talk, Ariel plays music. Trinculo and Stephano are afraid of the sound, but Caliban reassures them. The whole island is full of strange music, he says.

A spirit-feast

Ariel has more spectacular tricks to come. As Alonso and his lords come near Prospero's cell, there is more strange music. Prospero's spirits carry in a table and a wonderful banquet. They dance around it making courtly bows, and invite the lords to eat. Then they vanish.

Isle of music

Be not afeard: the isle is full of noises,
Sounds and sweet airs, that give delight, and hurt not.
Sometimes a thousand twangling instruments
Will hum about mine ears; and sometimes voices,
That, if I then had wak'd after long sleep,
Will make me sleep again: and then, in dreaming,
The clouds methought would open and show riches
Ready to drop upon me; that, when I wak'd
I cried to dream again.

Act III Sc ii

Their audience are all amazed. Sebastian and Antonio say they will believe all travellers' tales after this. The king is doubtful about eating, but the others persuade him. Then, as they approach the table, Ariel appears in a flash of lightning. He is dressed like a harpy (a legendary creature, half human, half bird), with huge black wings.

Three men of sin

Ariel tells Alonso, Sebastian and Antonio that they have been saved by destiny, so that they can suffer for their crimes. They cannot hurt him or his spirits; if they try, they will be unable to lift their swords. The elements have taken Ferdinand, because all creation is enraged with their wicked deeds. Only repentance can save them from a long, slow death on the island.

Ariel vanishes in a thunderclap, and his spirit helpers mockingly take away the banquet. Prospero, watching, is pleased. All his enemies are in his power.

They have all gone mad. Antonio and Sebastian try to fight the invisible spirits, while Alonso can think only of the dark, deep sea.

23

The masque of Juno

Prospero has more to do before he can reclaim his dukedom. Quickly he goes to Ferdinand and Miranda, and gives his blessing to their engagement. He summons Ariel for one last display of magic. It is his wedding-present to the young couple: a masque.

Three beautiful Greek goddesses appear: Iris, the messenger and goddess of the rainbow: Ceres, goddess of the harvest; and Juno, queen of the gods. They talk about the forthcoming wedding and bless Ferdinand and Miranda, while nymphs and reapers dance.

'Our revels now are ended'

Suddenly Prospero remembers Caliban's plot against him. He dismisses the dancers, explaining that they were nothing but his spirits in disguise. Now he must think how to deal with Caliban.

Life is a play
Be cheerful, sir:
Our revels now are ended. These our actors,
As I foretold you, were all spirits and
Are melted into air, into thin air:
And, like the baseless fabric of this vision,
The cloud-capp'd towers, the gorgeous palaces,
The solemn temples, the great globe itself,
Yea, all which it inherit, shall dissolve
And, like this insubstantial pageant faded,
Leave not a rack behind. We are such stuff
As dreams are made on, and our little life
Is rounded with a sleep.

Act IV Sc i

He asks Ariel to take rich clothes from his cell, and hang them up in the wind. As the three drunkards stagger towards Prospero's cell, the finery catches Trinculo's eye. Soon he and Stephano are quarrelling over it. Caliban tries to turn their minds back to murder, but they do not listen. Suddenly Ariel and Prospero appear with a pack of hounds, to chase them to prison.

Prospero's last spell

Prospero is pleased with Ariel's work. It is nearly time to free the mischievous spirit. The king and the conspirators are mad and unable to move, bound in a spell. The other lords, especially old Gonzalo, are distraught with grief. Prospero promises to be merciful, so long as they are truly sorry for their evil deeds. While Ariel goes to release them and bring them to Prospero, the old sorcerer swears to give up magic, after one more spell.

The magician retires
I have bedimm'd
The noontide sun, call'd forth the mutinous winds,
And 'twixt the green sea and the azur'd vault
Set roaring war: to the dread-rattling thunder
Have I given fire and rifted Jove's stout oak
With his own bolt: the strong-bas'd promontory
Have I made shake; and by the spurs pluck'd up
The pine and cedar: graves at my command
Have wak'd their sleepers, op'd, and let them forth
By my so potent art. But this rough magic
I here abjure; . . . I'll break my staff,
Bury it certain fathoms in the earth,
And, deeper than did ever plummet sound,
I'll drown my book.

Act v Sc i

To solemn music, Prospero restores his prisoners to their senses. As he frees each one, he reminds them of their crimes. Now he takes off his sorcerer's robes, and dresses in his old clothes, as a duke.

Lost and found

Alonso recognises him, and at once begs forgiveness. He asks to hear how Prospero came to be on the island, and tells him that he has lost his son. Prospero says he has lost a daughter too.

Then he lifts the curtain of his cell, to reveal Ferdinand and Miranda, playing chess. Alonso at first thinks it is another of the island's wonders; but soon realises it is true. Miranda stares astonished at all the people outside.

> **Mankind**
>
> Mira. *O, wonder!*
>   *How many goodly*
>   *creatures are*
>   *there here!*
>   *How beauteous*
>   *mankind is! O*
>   *brave new world,*
>   *That has such*
>   *people in't!*
> Pro. *'Tis new to thee.*
>   Act v Sc i

While everyone talks of the wedding, Ariel brings the ship's master and boatswain to the cell. They tell how they woke from deep sleep to find all the crew alive and the ship unscathed. Next come Caliban, Stephano and Trinculo. Prospero gives the king back his servants and sends Caliban to tidy his cell. Caliban, relieved not to be beaten, goes willingly. 'What a thrice double ass was I to take this drunkard for a god!'

Prospero says goodbye

Prospero sends the lords to his cell to spend the night. In the morning they will all set sail for Naples. Once Ariel has given them a following wind, he will be free. Alone, the old magician speaks direct to the audience. It is up to them whether he can go to Naples or not. Now he has no spells to help him, he needs their applause to send him on his way.

Epilogue
Now my charms are all o'erthrown,
And what strength I have's mine own;
Which is most faint: now, 'tis true,
I must be here confin'd by you,
Or sent to Naples. . . .

. . .

As you from crimes would pardon'd be,
Let your indulgence set me free.

The play's characters

Prospero

Prospero is a powerful figure, in three ways: as a magician, who can control spirits and the forces of nature; as a ruler (although, at the beginning of the play, he has lost his power as Duke of Milan, he rules the island); and as a father. He uses his power severely, as Caliban, Ariel and Ferdinand all learn. As duke, he was too trusting, and he is determined not to make the same mistake again. But sometimes he is hard on people to test them: once he knows that Ferdinand really loves Miranda, his severity melts away. His tenderness to Miranda shows a gentler side of his character. At the end, when he regains his rightful place as duke, he is able to be merciful.

Miranda

Miranda knows hardly anything of the world beyond the island; she can just remember the nursery-maids who looked after her when she was a tiny child. To her, Ferdinand and the other people from the ship are more extraordinary and marvellous than Ariel and Prospero's other spirits are to the audience. She

Prospero's nobility

Yet with my nobler reason 'gainst my fury
Do I take part: the rarer action is
In virtue than in vengeance: they being penitent,
The sole drift of my purpose doth extend
Not a frown further.

Act v Sc i

Ferdinand   Miranda   Prospero

Ferdinand on Prospero

O! she is ten times more gentle
than her father's crabbed,
And he's compos'd of harshness.

Act iii Sc i

Miranda on her father

My father's of a better nature,
sir,
Than he appears by speech:

Act i Sc ii

28

Ariel

has the innocence of a romantic heroine, but she also has a tough and determined side to her character. When she tells Ferdinand, 'I'll be your servant, whether you will or no', we know that she means what she says.

Ferdinand
A brave young romantic hero, Ferdinand willingly accepts slavery when it means he is near the beautiful Miranda. He is unaware of his father's part in the plot against Prospero, and so, having none of Alonso's guilt, does not share his gloomy side. His love for Miranda is consolation for all the troubles he suffers.

Ariel
As his name suggests, Ariel is a spirit of the air: one of the 'four elements' which, according to the philosophy of the time, made up the universe and governed people's characters. Everything about him is light and mobile; he longs to be free, like the wind. He is a mischievous spirit, who cannot resist playing a joke on Caliban, Stephano and Trinculo even if it means putting off the work that Prospero has given him. But he knows where to draw the line and is careful not to provoke his master's anger.

Caliban
Caliban is a creature of the earth – the opposite of the air among the four elements. (The others are fire and water.) Though he is surly, and cannot take his position as Prospero's slave as lightly as Ariel, there are some warm and sympathetic sides to his character. He obviously loves the island, both its natural riches and the strange supernatural music which the spirits make, and knows it better than anyone. Like Miranda, he knows nothing of the world beyond, and is overwhelmed with admiration when he meets someone from it.

Caliban

Alonso

Antonio

Sebastian

Villainy

You are three men of sin, whom Destiny–
That hath to instrument this lower world
And what is in't, – the never-surfeited sea
Hath caused to belch up you; and on this island
Where man doth not inhabit; you 'mongst men
Being most unfit to live.

Act III Sc iii

Gonzalo

I would with such perfection
  govern, sir,
To excel the golden age.

Act II Sc i

Though a comical figure, an old man who talks endlessly, Gonzalo is still a very sympathetic character. He is an optimist, who always sees the best in people and events, and though he takes this to ridiculous lengths sometimes, it is hard not to warm to him. He saved Prospero's and Miranda's lives when they were banished, and though his dream of a perfect society is impossible, as Antonio and Sebastian point out, it is a better ideal than their quest for power.

Alonso

The King of Naples is a sad and guilty man. Even before he learns that he has actually landed on Prospero's island, he feels that the shipwreck, and the death (as he thinks) of his son and heir, are a punishment for his part in Antonio's conspiracy. As the play proceeds, he becomes more and more helpless, sunk in grief and guilt. Nothing can raise him from despair, until he learns that Prospero and Ferdinand are both alive, and he has the chance to make amends.

Antonio and Sebastian

The brothers of Prospero (Antonio) and Alonso (Sebastian) are two of many wicked brothers in Shakespeare's plays. Besides their ruthless desire for power, even planning to kill their fellow-conspirator Alonso, they are cruel to others, such as Gonzalo, for fun. Unlike Alonso, they feel no guilt at all, and are angry and sullen when released from Prospero's final spell.

Gonzalo

The life and plays of Shakespeare

Life of Shakespeare

1564 William Shakespeare born at Stratford-upon-Avon.

1582 Shakespeare marries Anne Hathaway, eight years his senior.

1583 Shakespeare's daughter, Susanna, is born.

1585 The twins, Hamnet and Judith, are born.

1587 Shakespeare goes to London.

1591-2 Shakespeare writes *The Comedy of Errors*. He is becoming well-known as an actor and writer.

1592 Theatres closed because of plague.

1593-4 Shakespeare writes *Titus Andronicus* and *The Taming of the Shrew*: he is member of the theatrical company, the Chamberlain's Men.

1594-5 Shakespeare writes *Romeo and Juliet*.

1595 Shakespeare writes *A Midsummer Night's Dream*.

1595-6 Shakespeare writes *Richard II*.

1596 Shakespeare's son, Hamnet, dies. He writes *King John* and *The Merchant of Venice*.

1597 Shakespeare buys New Place in Stratford.

1597-8 Shakespeare writes *Henry IV*.

1599 Shakespeare's theatre company opens the Globe Theatre.

1599-1600 Shakespeare writes *As You Like It*, *Henry V* and *Twelfth Night*.

1600-01 Shakespeare writes *Hamlet*.

1602-03 Shakespeare writes *All's Well That Ends Well*.

1603 Elizabeth I dies. James I becomes king. Theatres closed because of plague.

1603-04 Shakespeare writes *Othello*.

1605 Theatres closed because of plague.

1605-06 Shakespeare writes *Macbeth* and *King Lear*.

1606-07 Shakespeare writes *Antony and Cleopatra*.

1607 Susanna Shakespeare marries Dr John Hall. Theatres closed because of plague.

1608 Shakespeare's granddaughter, Elizabeth Hall, is born.

1609 *Sonnets* published. Theatres closed because of plague.

1610 Theatres closed because of plague. Shakespeare gives up his London lodgings and retires to Stratford.

1611-12 Shakespeare writes *The Tempest*.

1613 Globe Theatre burns to the ground during a performance of Henry VIII.

1616 Shakespeare dies on 23 April.

Shakespeare's plays

The Comedy of Errors
Love's Labour's Lost
Henry VI Part 2
Henry VI Part 3
Henry VI Part 1
Richard III
Titus Andronicus
The Taming of the Shrew
The Two Gentlemen of Verona
Romeo and Juliet
Richard II
A Midsummer Night's Dream
King John
The Merchant of Venice
Henry IV Part 1
Henry IV Part 2
Much Ado About Nothing
Henry V
Julius Caesar
As You Like It
Twelfth Night
Hamlet
The Merry Wives of Windsor
Troilus and Cressida
All's Well That Ends Well
Othello
Measure for Measure
King Lear
Macbeth
Antony and Cleopatra
Timon of Athens
Coriolanus
Pericles
Cymbeline
The Winter's Tale
The Tempest
Henry VIII

Index

Numerals in *italics* refer to picture captions.

Acknowledgements
The publishers would like to thank Morag Gibson for her help in producing this book.

Picture credits
p.3 Peter Newark's American Pictures, p.4, 5 The Mansell Collection, p.6 Peter Newark's American Pictures, p.8 & p9 Mary Evans Picture Library, p.10 The Kobal Collection.